Who Has Whiskers?

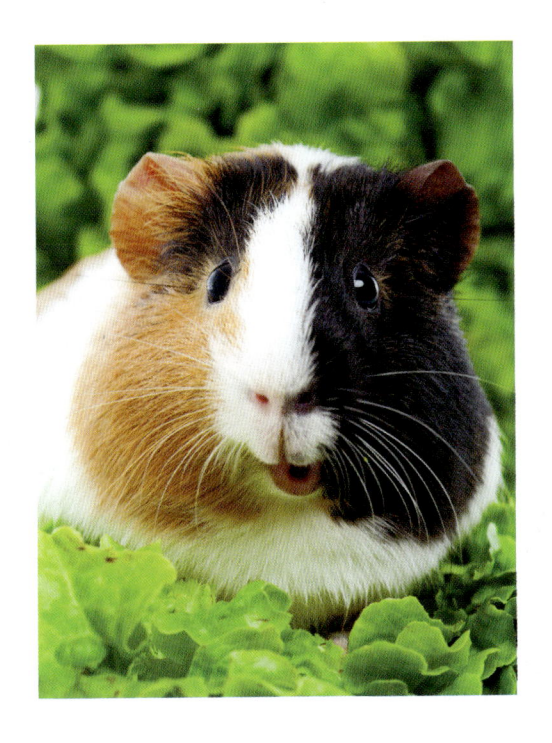

written by Pam Holden

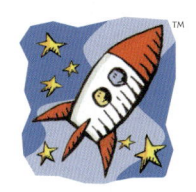

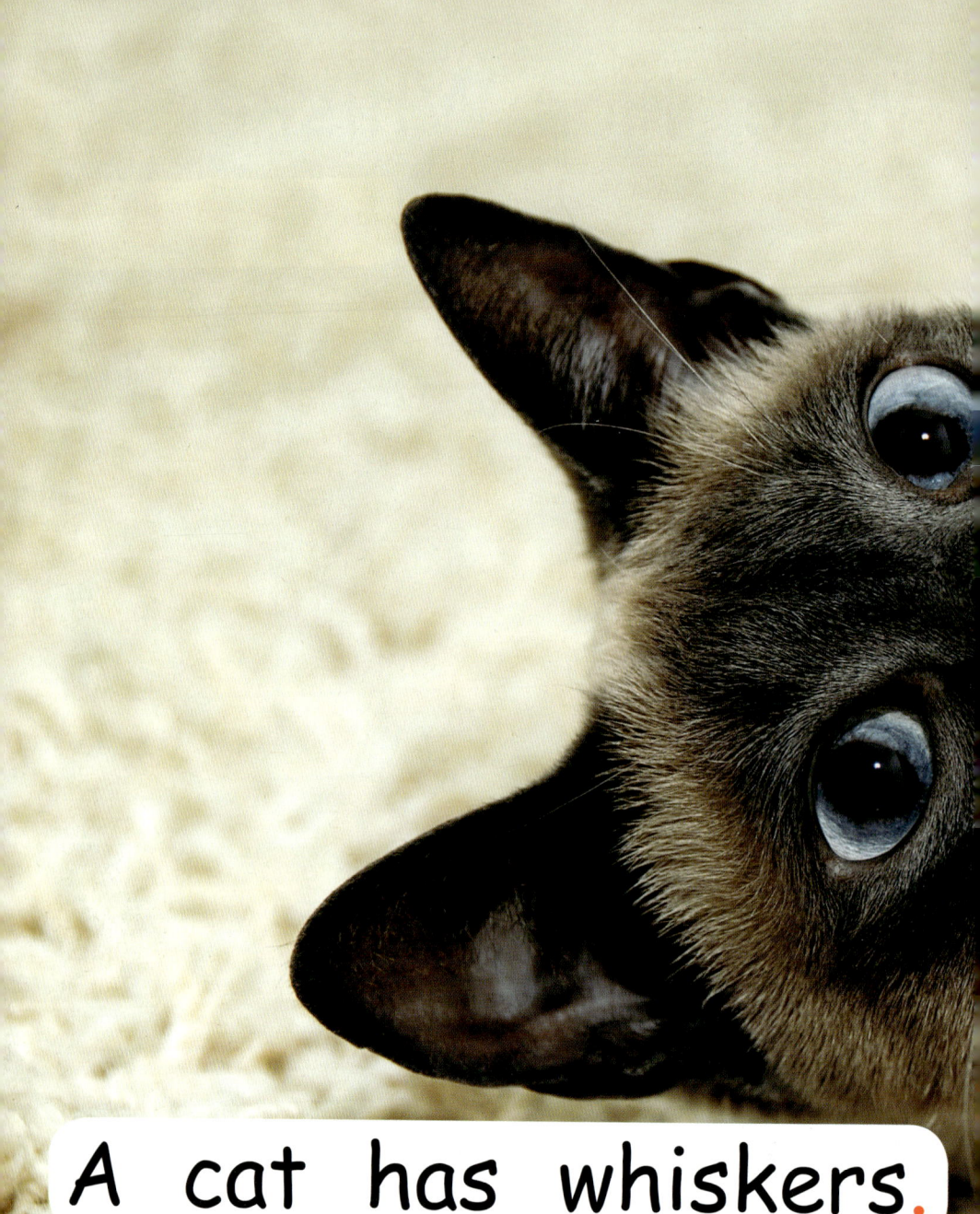

A cat has whiskers.

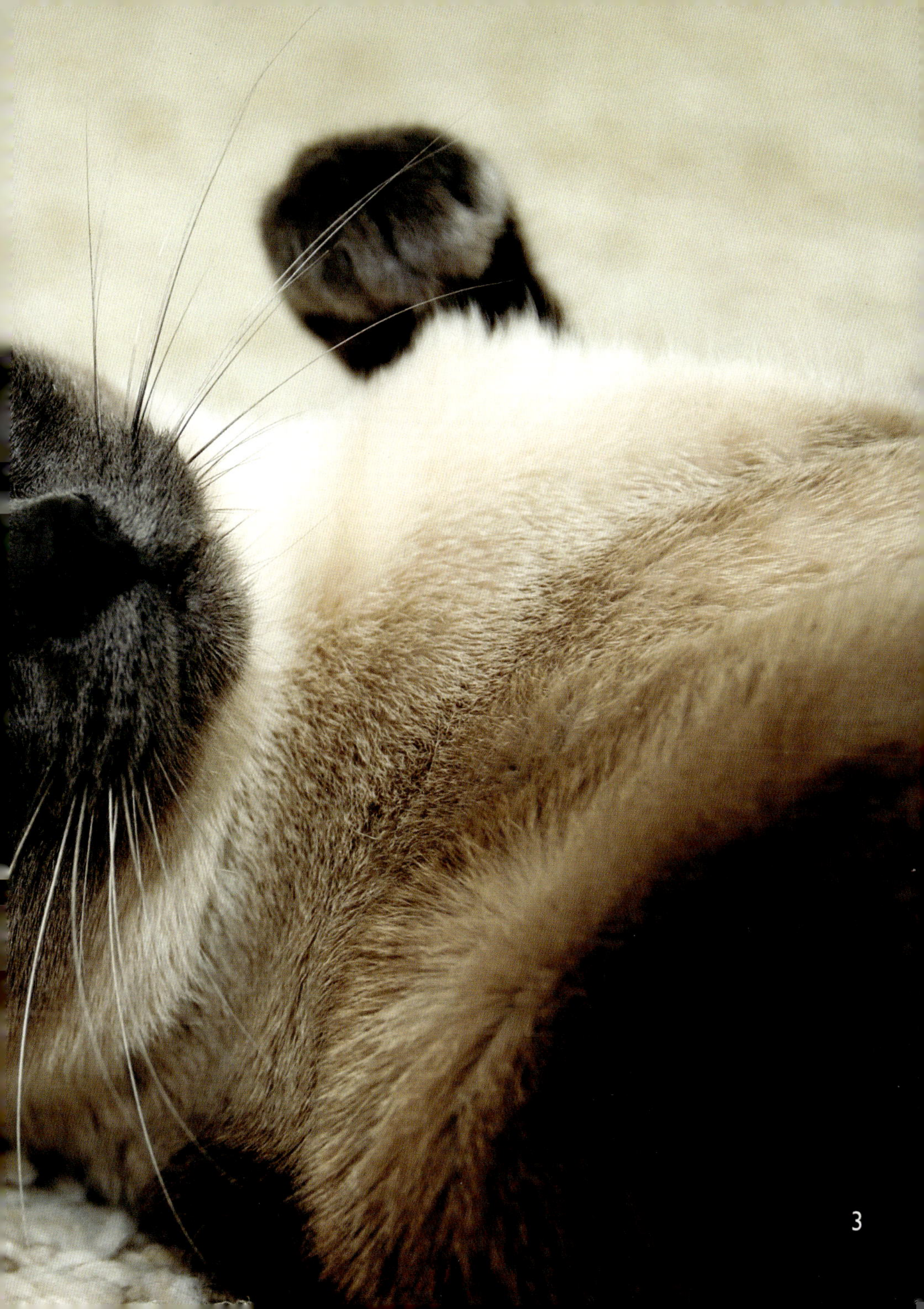

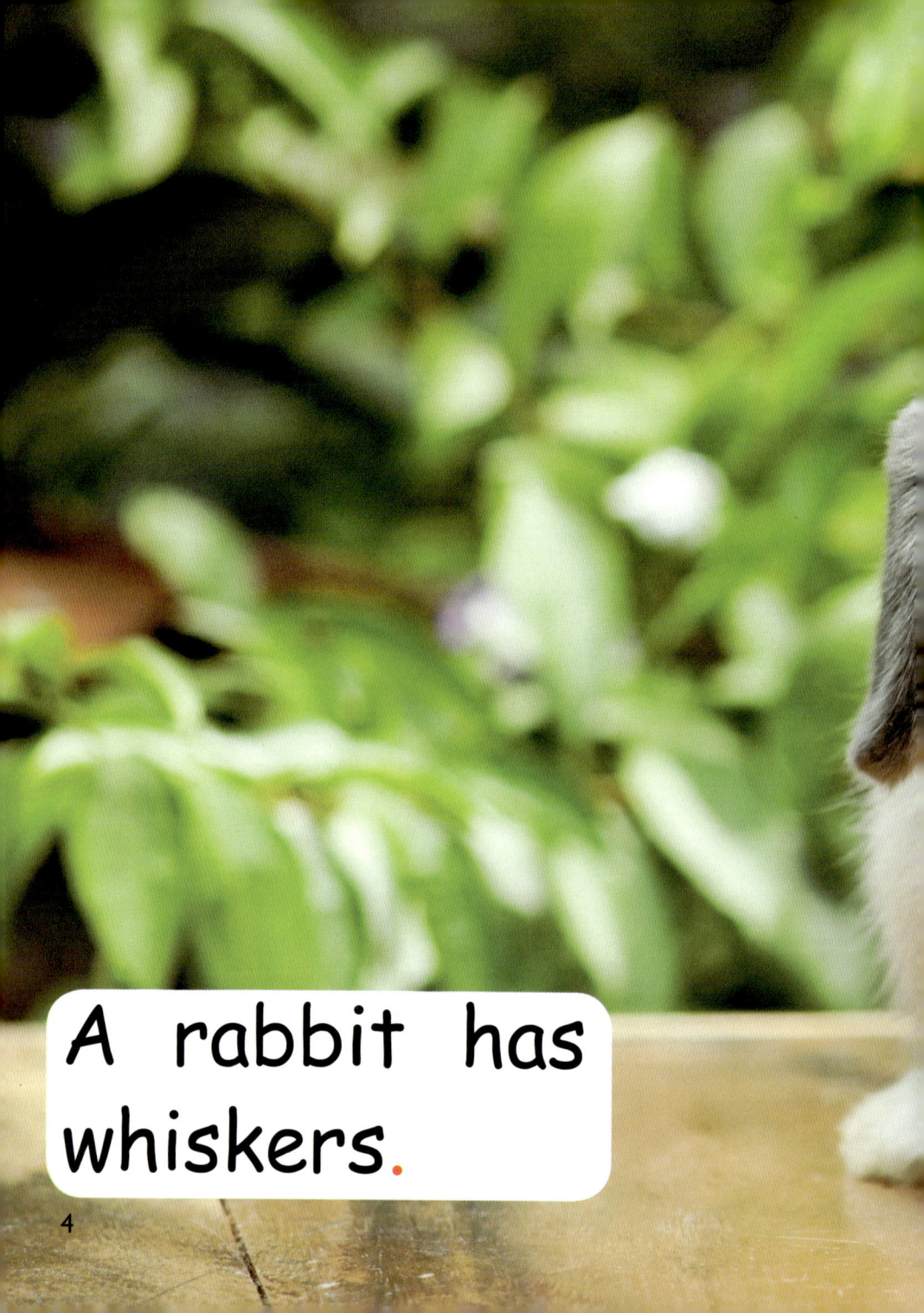

A rabbit has whiskers.

5

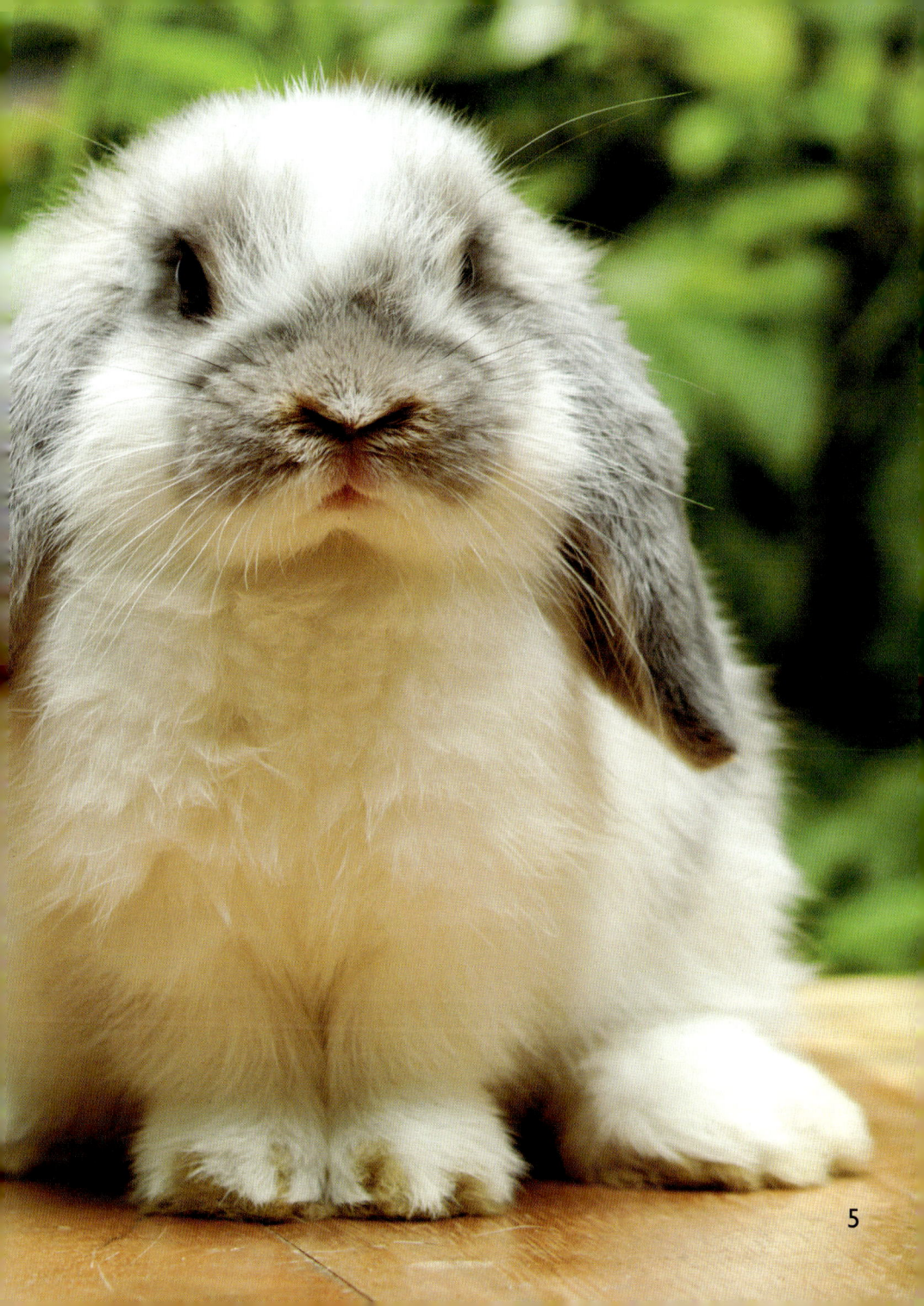

A dog has whiskers.

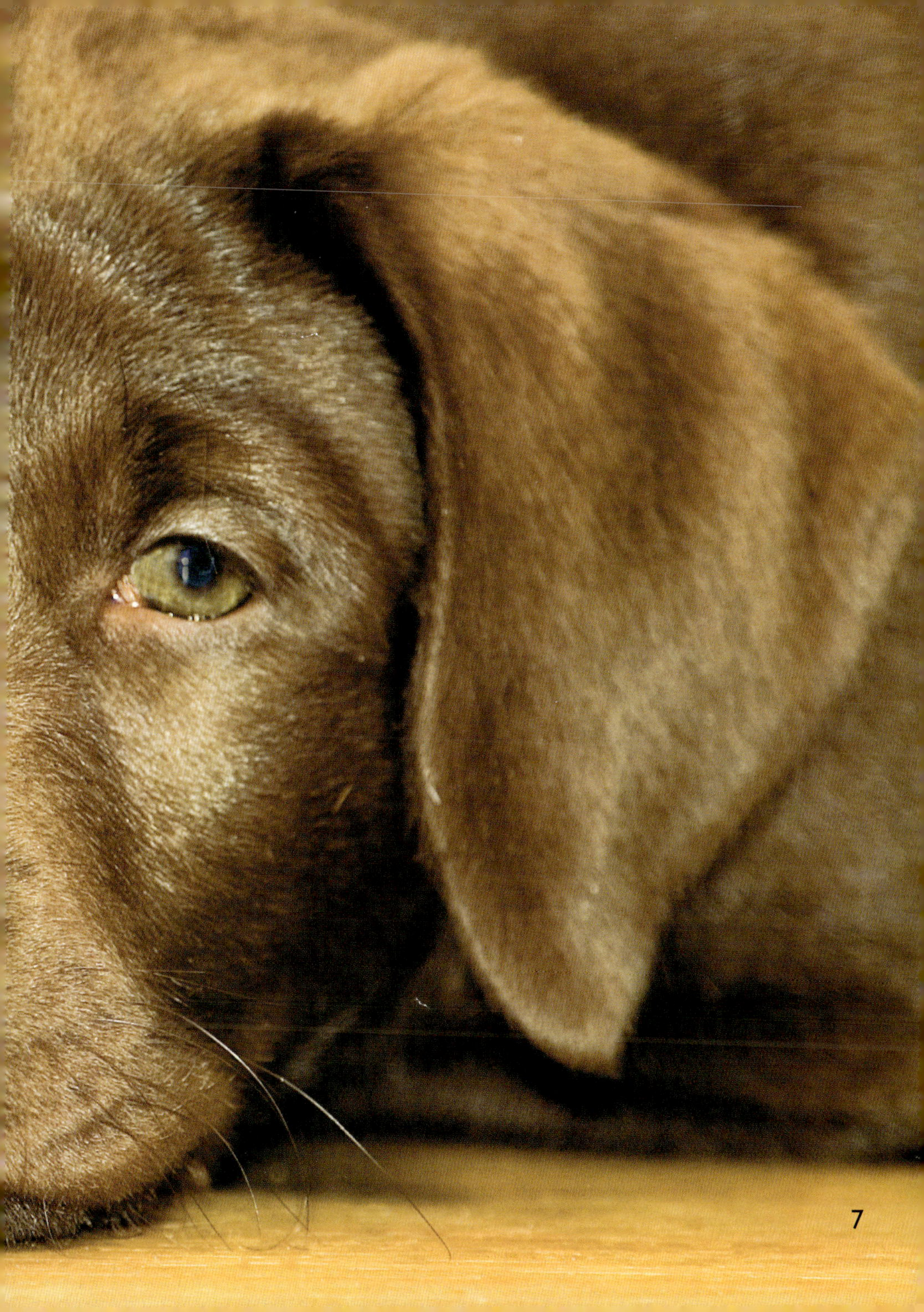

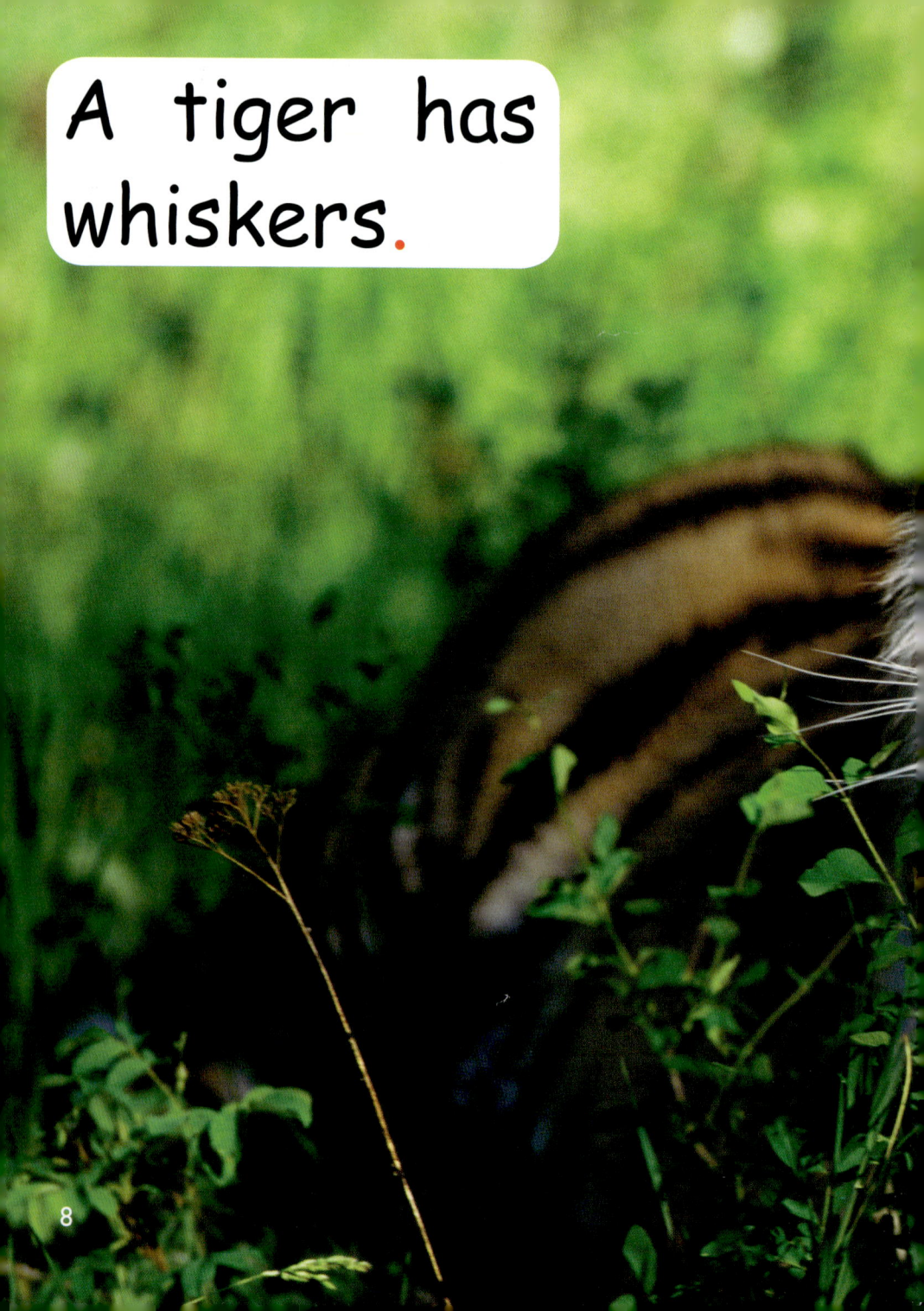

A tiger has whiskers.

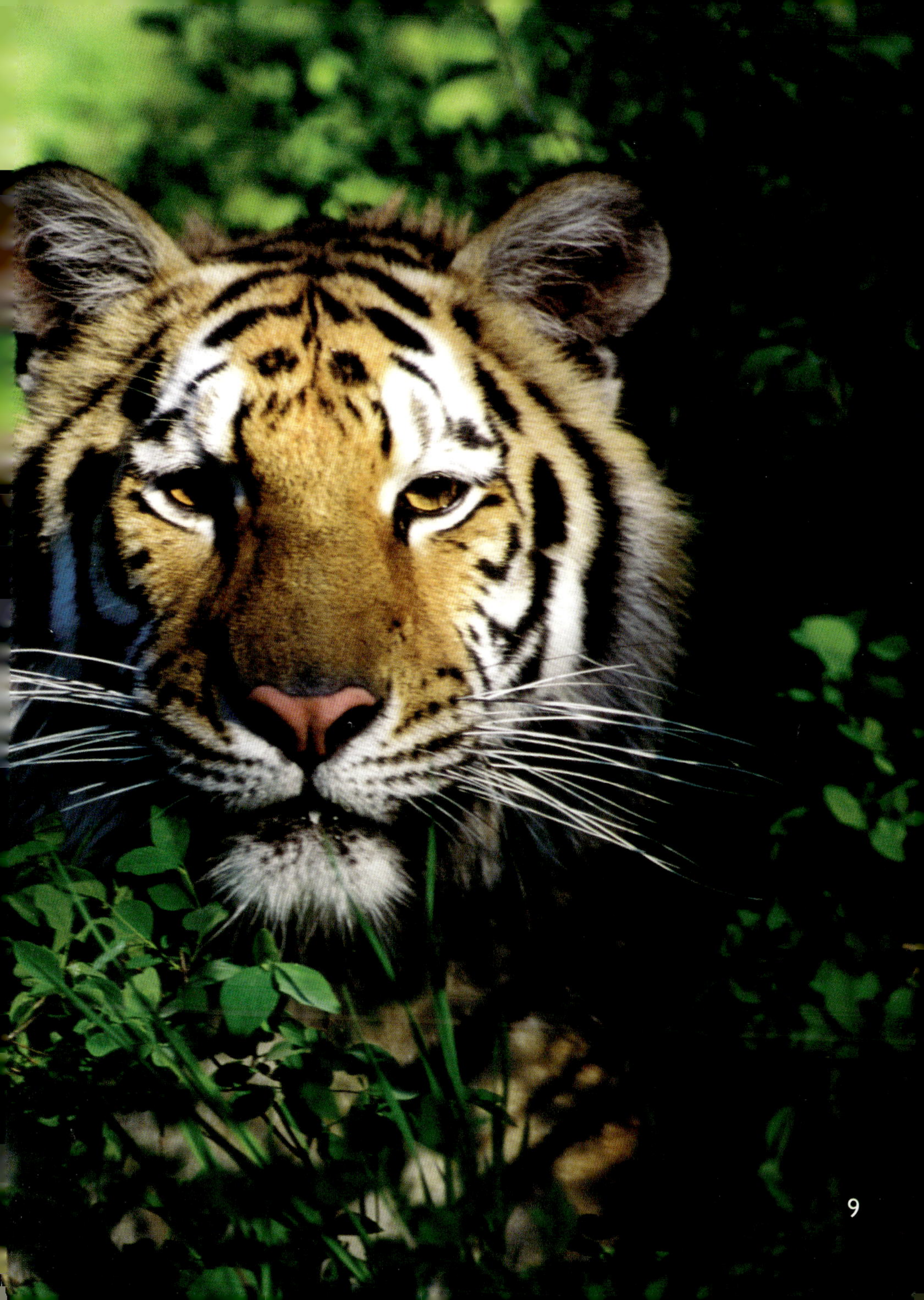

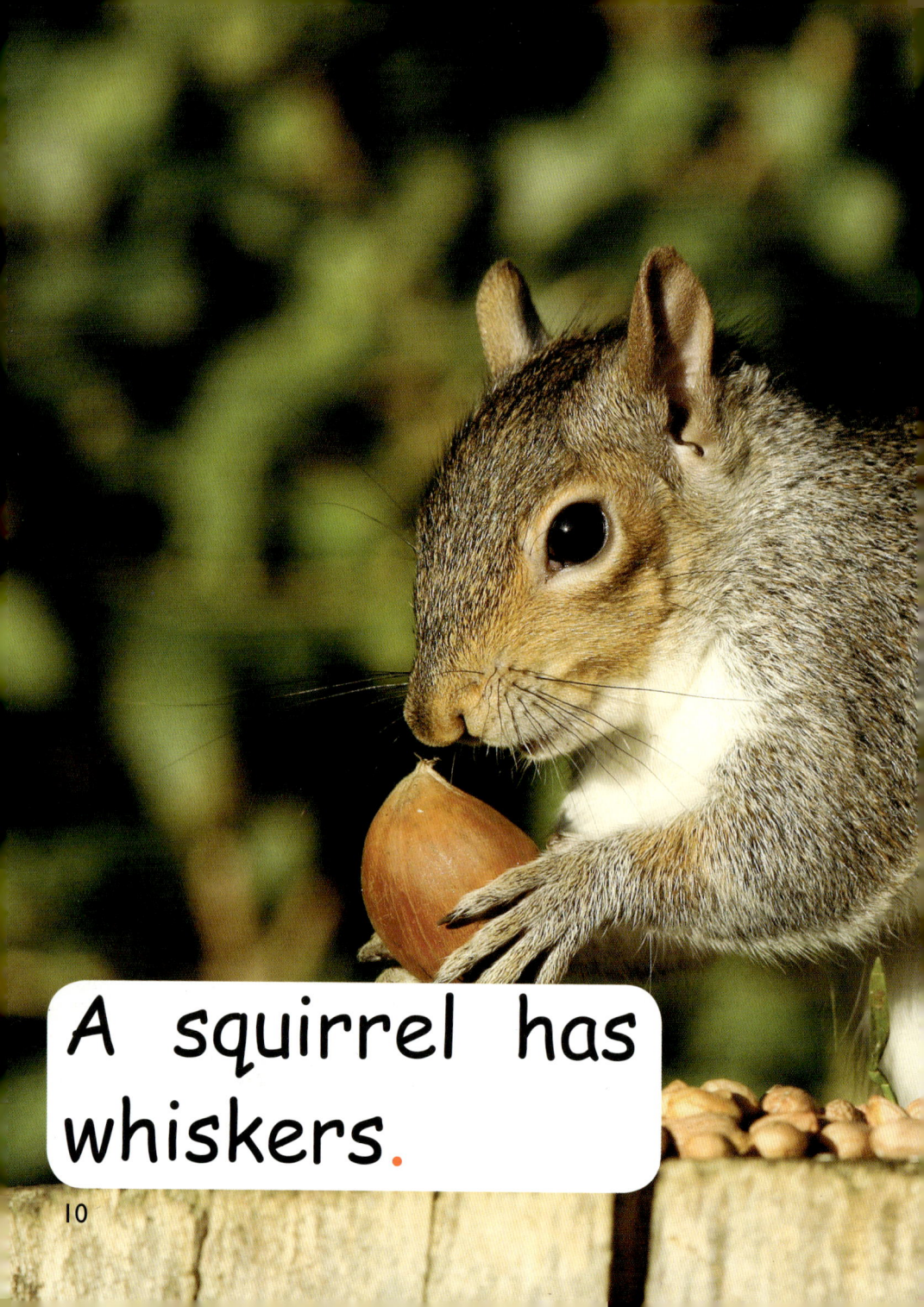

A squirrel has whiskers.

11

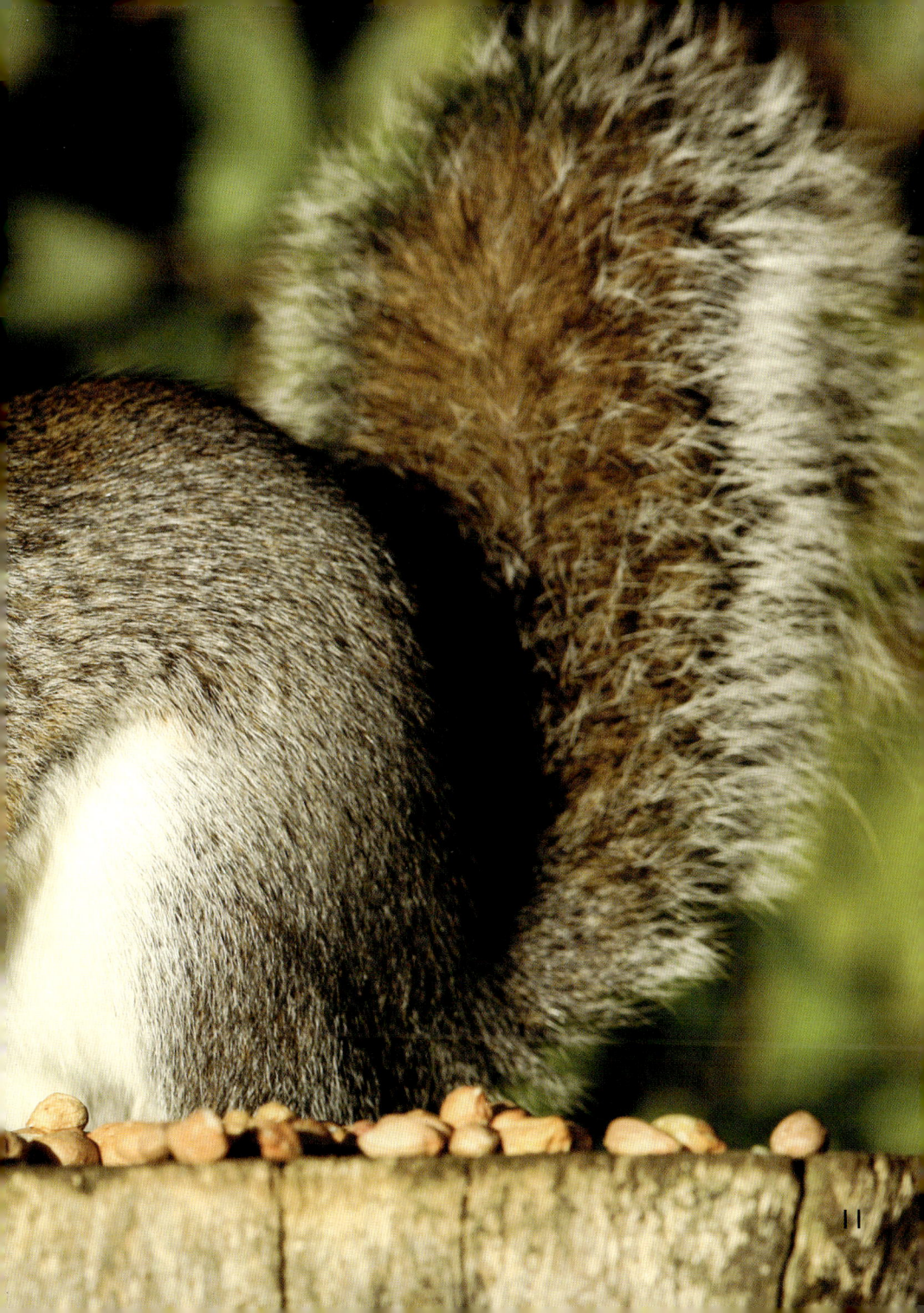

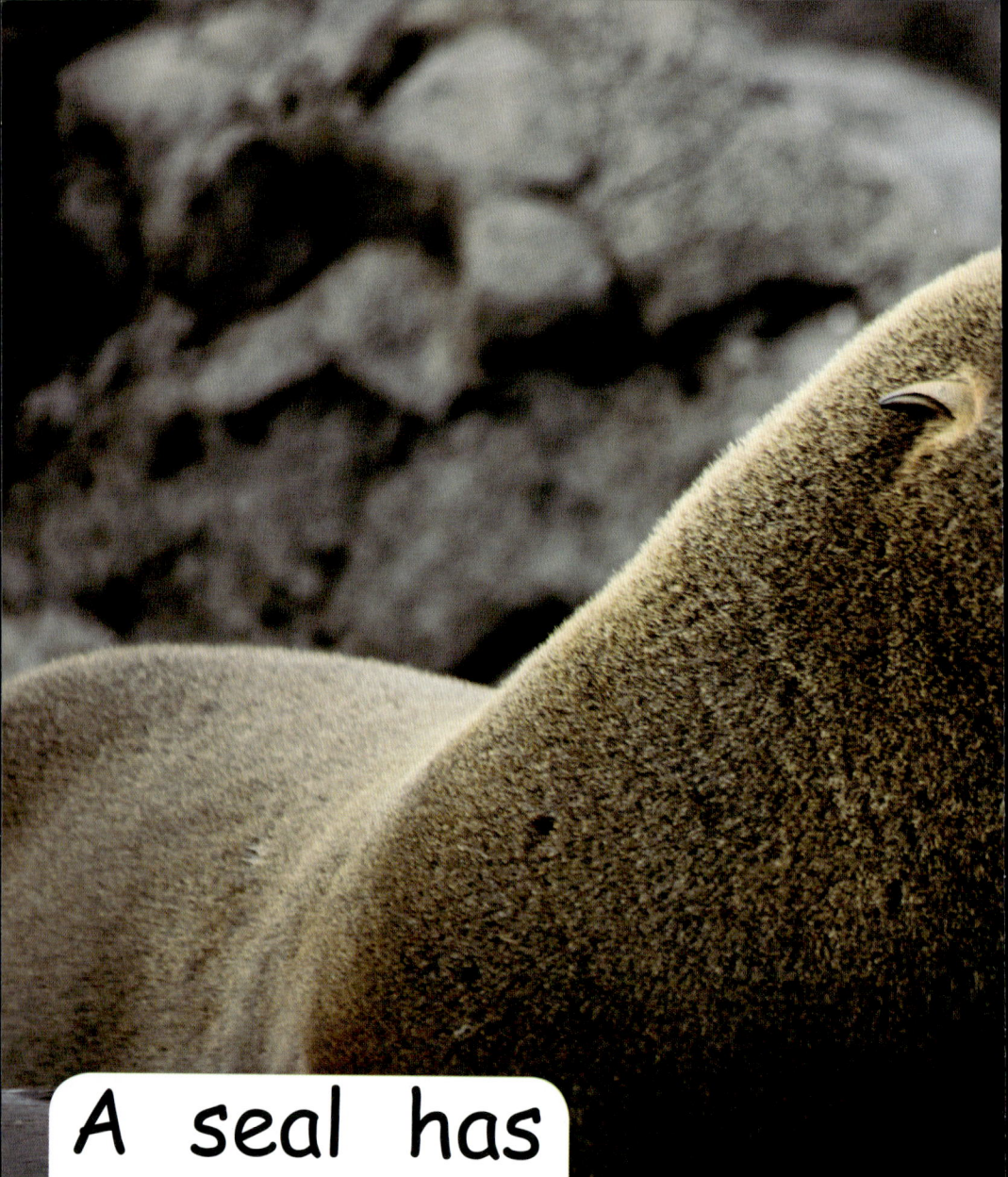

A seal has whiskers.

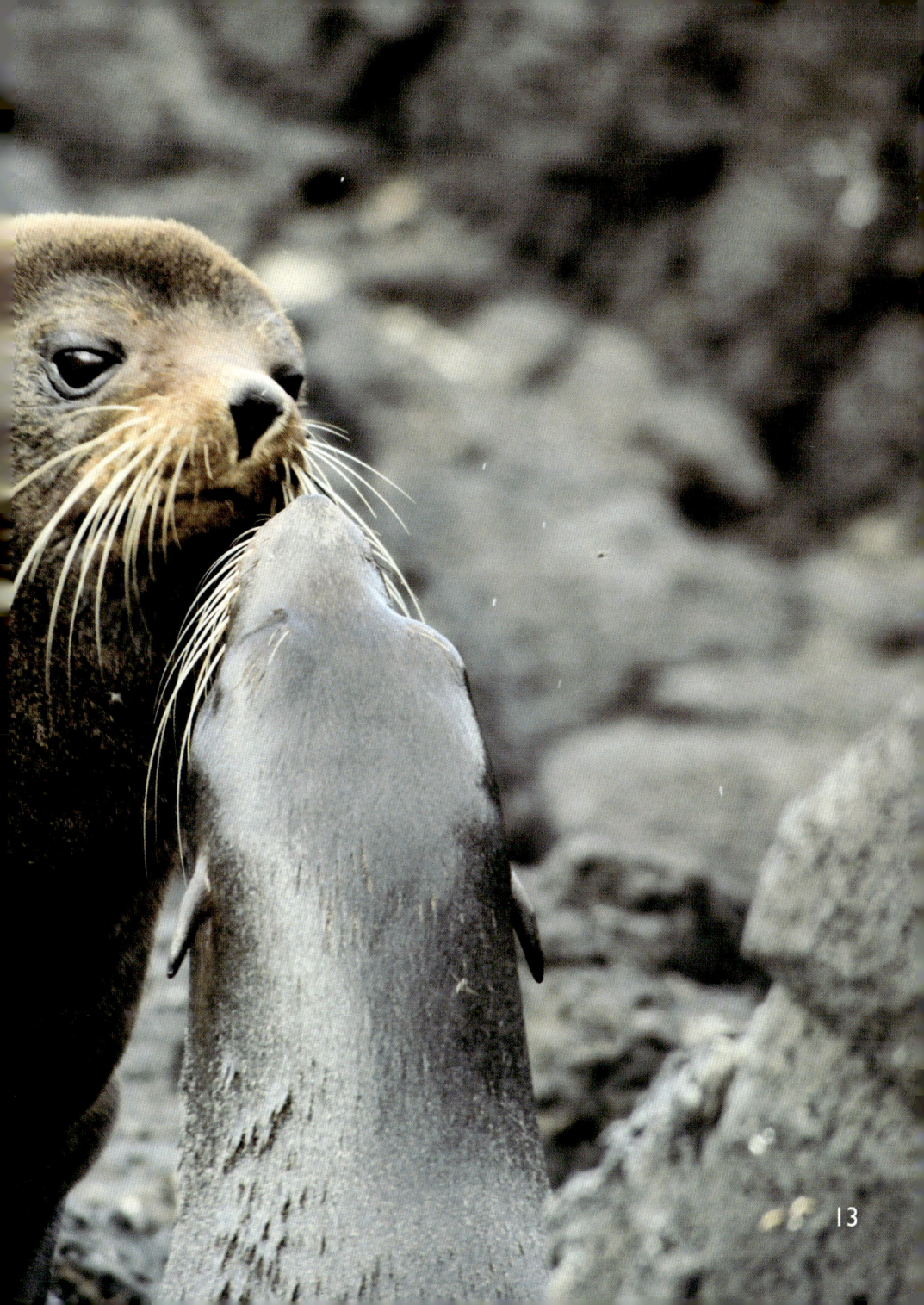

A mouse has whiskers.

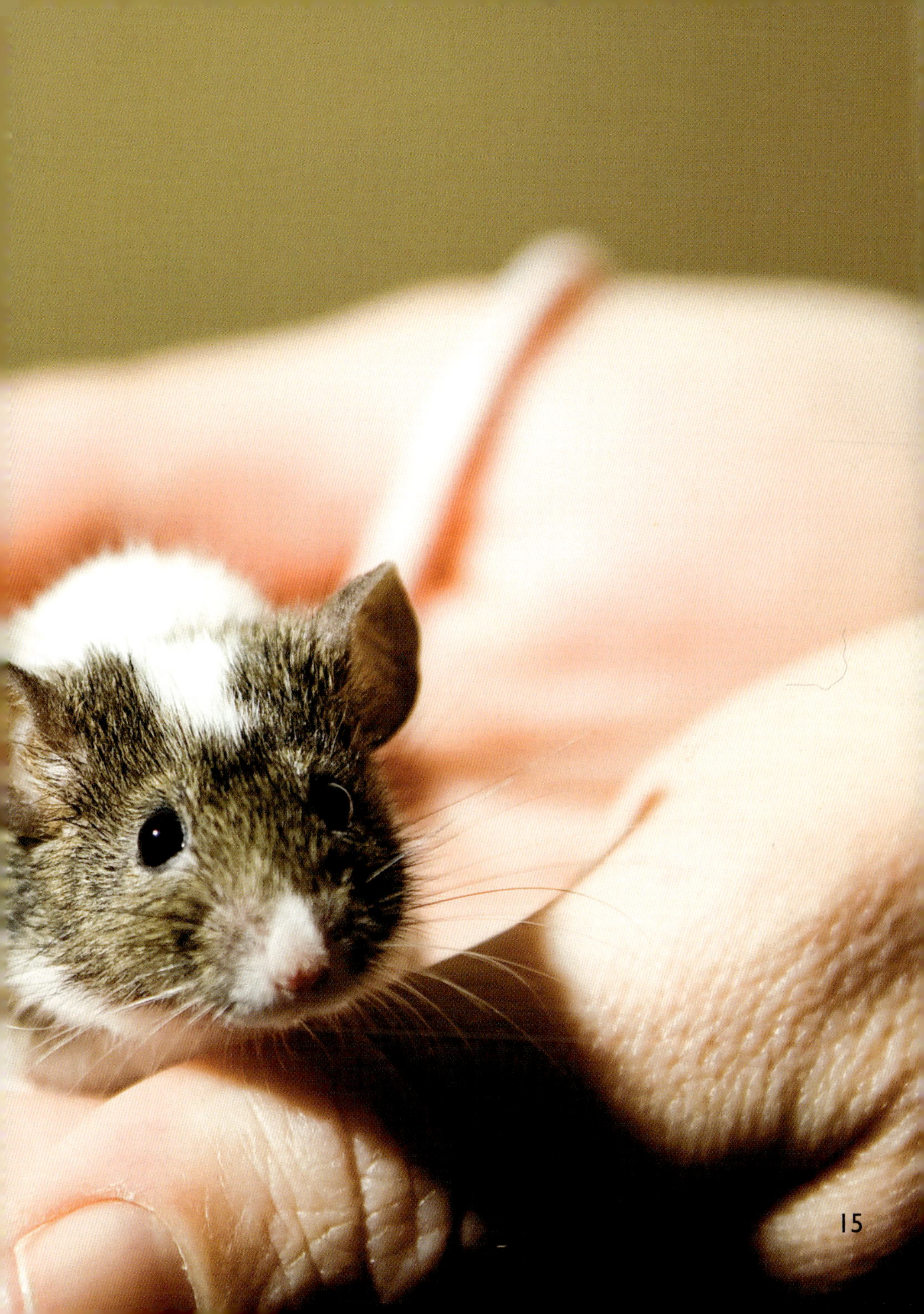

A lion has whiskers.

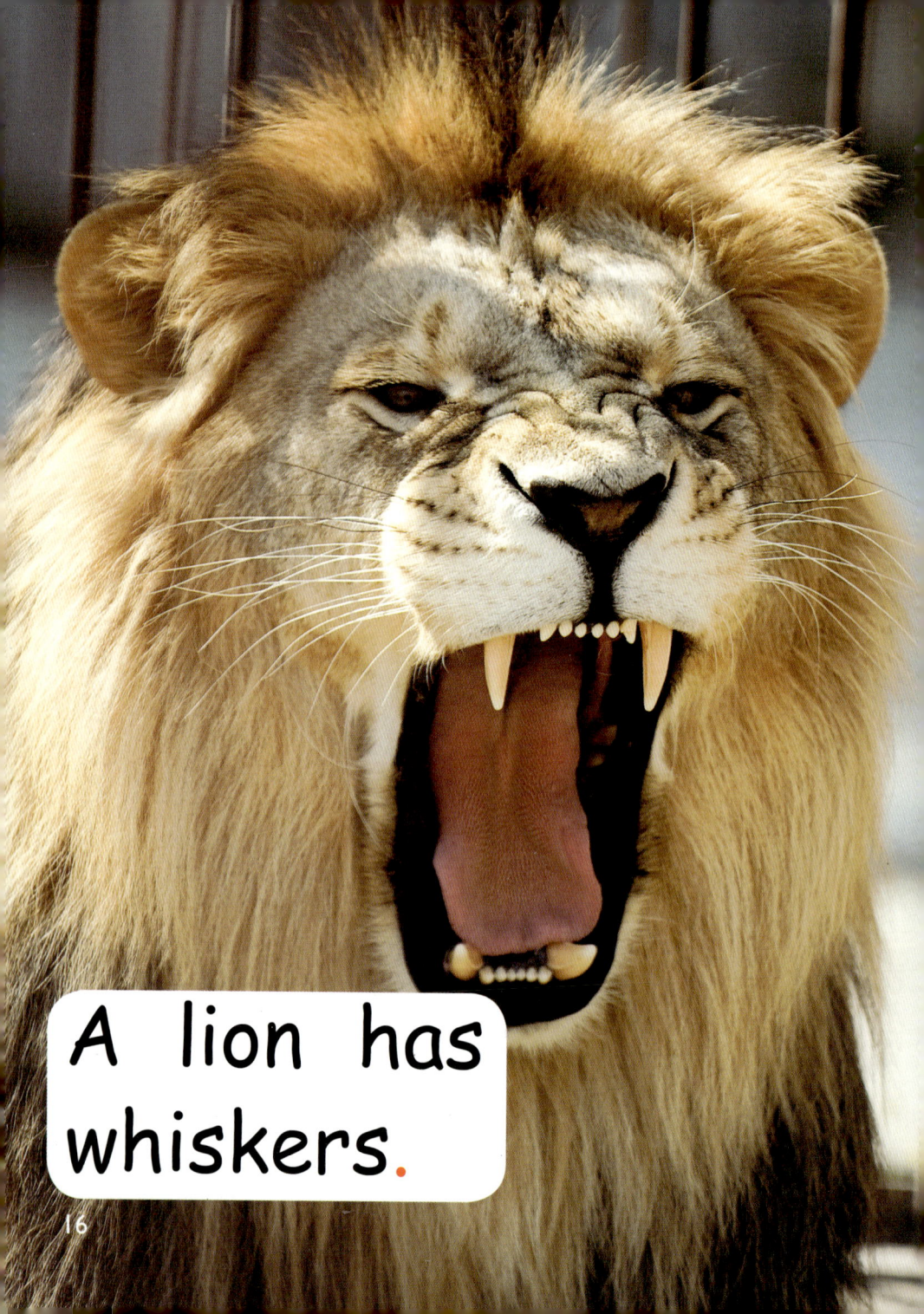